wit and wisdom

wit and wisdom

inspirational thoughts on life

edited by toby reynolds

Published in the United States in 2005
by Tangent Publications
an imprint of
Axis Publishing Limited
8c Accommodation Road
London NW11 8ED
www.axispublishing.co.uk

Creative Director: Siân Keogh
Editorial Director: Anne Yelland
Production Manager: Jo Ryan

ISBN 1–904707–24–6

2 4 6 8 10 9 7 5 3 1

Printed and bound in China

about this book

This is a collection of funny and quirky sayings designed to make you smile. It's a book to keep to hand for those "Aaarh!" moments when nothing seems to be going right and what you really need is to take five and calm down: these sayings will help you to see the funny side.

Attractively illustrated with amusing animal photographs, *Wit and Wisdom* is an ideal gift book and an inspired self-purchase for anyone who feels life is just too much at the moment.

about the author

Toby Reynolds is an experienced editor and author who has been involved in publishing for more than a decade. From the many hundreds of contributions that were sent to him, he has selected the ones that will make you smile, cheer your spirits, and generally make you see the lighter side of life.

To come home from the casino with a small fortune, go to the casino with a large one.

The best way to double your money? Fold it over.

Money can't buy happiness,
but it can buy you the kind
of misery you prefer.

I am having an out of money experience.

If it draws blood, it's hardware.

RAM disk is not an
installation procedure.

It's easier to get into
almost anything than to
get out of it.

Computers can
work out a lot of
things, except
things that just
don't add up.

Don't force it…

…get a larger hammer.

If you don't know what you're doing, call it research.

When working toward the
solution to a problem,
it usually helps to know
the answer.

If an experiment works,
something has gone wrong.

Soccer: a game where a few fit men run around for an hour and a half while people who could use the exercise watch them.

It's great that exercise kills germs, but how do you get the germs to exercise in the first place?

It's impossible to make anything foolproof because fools are so ingenious.

The piece that wasn't in the box is the piece that supports 90 percent of the rest of the box's contents.

If you're good, you'll get given the project. If you're really good, you'll get out of it.

Any system which relies
on human reliability
is unreliable.

The opulence of the front office decor is inversely proportional to a company's solvency.

The more pretentious
the company name,
the smaller the company.

No great ideas were
ever born in a conference,
but a lot of dumb ones
died there.

When you don't
want to do anything,
have a meeting.

No-one rings in sick
on Wednesdays.

Meetings are things
where minutes are kept
and hours are lost.

If you're shopping on-line,
your boss will stop by
your desk and ask you to
do something.

A person's importance is inversely proportional to the number of pens on his desk.

Useless legislation: the law forbidding a man from marrying his mother-in-law.

We childproofed the house
two years ago…

…unfortunately the kids
are still getting in.

A teenager is always too tired to hold a dishcloth, but never too tired to hold a telephone.

If practice makes perfect
and nobody's perfect,
why practice?

Multi-tasking: messing everything up at the same time.

By the time the guy arrives to fix the xerox machine, it will be working perfectly again.

Anything you do can get you fired. This includes doing nothing.

I've got all the money
I'll ever need…

…unless I buy something.

I don't need much money
—just enough to tide me
over until
I need some more.

I don't understand why there is so much month left at the end of the money.

Logic: a systematic method of confidently reaching the wrong conclusion.

If you can't laugh
at yourself, others will
do it for you.

Exceptions prove
the rule…

…and wreck the budget.

The best things in life are free, and worth every penny.

Only those who dare
to fail greatly can ever
achieve greatly.

Freedom is not worth having if it does not include the freedom to make mistakes.

Success seems to be largely a matter of hanging on after others have let go.

One thing you
can't recycle is
wasted time.

If you don't learn to laugh at troubles, you won't have anything to laugh at when you grow old.

If I promise to miss you,
will you go away?

The amount of
sleep needed by the
average person is five
minutes more.

The fact that no-one understands you doesn't make you an artist.

On the keyboard of life,
it pays to keep a finger
on the Escape key.

Children brighten a household…

…they never turn off the lights.

Procrastinate now…

…don't put it off.

Everything comes
to those who wait.

Worrying never
changed anything.

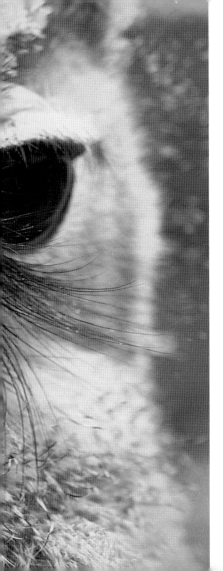

True wisdom
is to live in the
present, plan
for the future,
and profit from
the past.

Faith begins
where reason ends.

Money can't buy love, but it gives you a great bargaining position.

There are only ever two sizes in the stores: too large and too small.

However far you travel, you will never find the girl who smiles at you from the travel brochure.

The mark of a truly great salesman is that he can make his wife feel sorry for the girl who lost her underwear in his car.

If you're not living on the edge,
you're taking up too much space.